To

_____

From

_____

Upcoming Books by
Shakisha Shamain Edness

Women Overcoming Weight-loss Book
Women Overcoming Weight-loss Journal
Women Overcoming Weight-loss Workbook
Break Through Volume I & II
Break Through I & II Workbook
A Christmas to Remember
From the Eyes of a Child
A Man Can Only Do What a Woman Allows

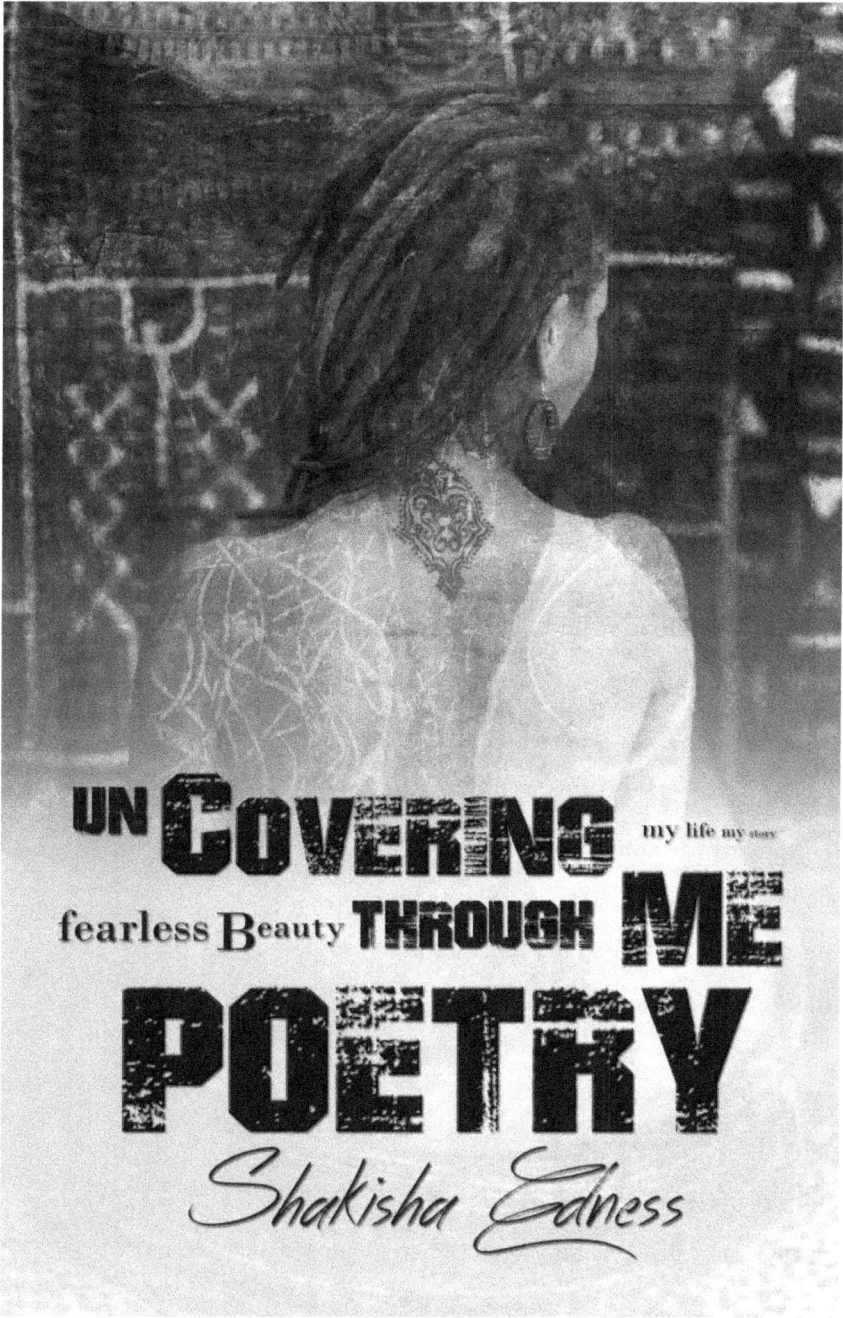

UN **COVERING** my life my story

fearless Beauty THROUGH ME

POETRY

Shakisha Edness

UNCOVERING ME THROUGH POETRY

Cover design: Jacobie Brown

Editor: Shanice Edness

Cover illustration: Google and Shutterstock

Interior illustration: Google and Shutterstock

Interior design: T.R.A.C Publishing

Bible Scriptures: New Living Translation

ISBN-10: 069225515X

ISBN-13: 978-0692255155

Library of Congress catalog card number:

Printed in the United States of America

Note to the Reader

I wrote *Uncovering Me through Poetry*, unaware of being gifted to write poetry.

I owe the inspiration to the distress I endured. When I gave birth to my children it was painful and this reminded me much of those labor pains.

During this time I desired to be married. I practiced celibacy for seven years and six months. But I found someone I chose to love, with him not having the same love towards me, grieved my spirit.

Through these poems you will undergo the different emotions I was on during this time.

Reflections of my past discovered other things I decided to expose. I pray this poetry ministers to many people emotionally, mentally, and spiritually.

I am a believer of the 'The Most High' God. Both non-believers and believers have sexual desires and hang ups; though many may not tell you to save face. This book shows that side of me.

I pray this book bless you and help you to uncover the Covered Potential that's in you.

Contents

Acknowledgements

I acknowledge my pain because it birthed Greatness through me! Many times I went from one fiery furnace to the next, one wilderness to another and not to mention the Lion's den but God!

So use me Lord the way you choose. I owe God the Praise in Jesus Name Amen...

Matthew Kirkland Jr., Thank you so much for being the first to acknowledge the little poet in me.

Orlanda P. Brown, Thank you for being used by God to help pull the poet into poetry. I will forever be grateful for you. Though it was painful for me, I endured and pressed. I love you and wish you the best!

I thank ***Tranisha Hollman, Shandra Smalls*** and ***Reginald Leonard*** for being true friends who've helped me through my grieving moments.

Richard B. Gibbs Jr. Thank you so much for being who you are to me, supportive, forever believing in me and always speaking words of encouragement to me. You've cooked, cleaned and never complained regardless to the extra responsibilities during this time so I thank you.

Larry Clifton Riley I am loss of words when I reminisce on how much you have inspired me to write in these last months. You have given me hope and even suggested titles to other books to write. Daddy you are the reason I sing! I love you...

Shukriyyah and **Shanice Edness,** my gorgeous daughters, thanks for loving me in spite of me and I pray this book bless you both!

A host of family and friends I love you and to name a few my siblings **Shakim** and **Shahidah Edness** may God bless you both!

My cousins **Tony Edness, Chico, Sonja** and **Marone Rodriguez** much love!

Women Overcoming Prayer Line for always lifting, supporting, encouraging me but more for being a listening ear and shoulder to cry on. I thank **Ilene** and **Cassandra Hollman, Anissha James Walton, Kristie Steele** and a host of others.

Sidney Smith, Jr. at an early age you taught me how to set goals and reach them. I owe this to you. Thank you daddy, I did it!

Dedication

I dedicate this book to myself. I finally tapped into the part of me that cries out and I allowed her to cry out loud. No more fears, shame or blame.

This book is truly me expressing the love that has been buried way deep but people have not allowed me to express this part of me.

So it laid dormant inside for many years, I promise these bones that were once dry are living again and shall live forever.

I extend this dedication to a man that stole my heart and broke it into pieces. Which caused me to put myself back together. I decided I will go on a treasure hunt.

The search showed me one man's scrap is another's man Jewel!

This book is parental advised because though its poetry; it's truly the naked side of me, so explicit it can be.

I, thank you **Shakisha Edness** for continuing to press toward the mark of the High Call!

Blessings!

Uncovering Me through Poetry

By Ms. Shakisha Edness

The Cake Date

He wants his cake and wants to eat it too,
I remember growing up hearing this about you;
He wants his cake and he wants to eat it too.
Well, I love cake and
If I order a slice I will want to eat it too.

Desert with your order?
Yes, of course.
Chocolate cake for me and strawberry shortcake for him.
Please, thank you.

I prefer chocolate and he prefers strawberry,
That's the diversity in this cake date.
He desires to remain single, sex with no strings attached.
I guess, I should ask am I really his match?

I want a commitment, engagement and a life-long companionship.
Though we're eating from the same table,
We cannot share off of the same plate
Because we both have total different tastes.

Here's your desert. Enjoy!
He responds "Yes, I will thank you and it's exactly the way I like it."

Is his cake good? Yes, I'm sure.
Is mine better? No just my preference.

But at the end of this date, the one thing we have in common is it's our
choice
To choose off the menu, that of which is pleasing and satisfying to us
individually.

I must be honest his strawberry shortcake looks pretty appetizing.
I can visualize me wrapping my lips around his spoon, closing my eyes
and
Enjoying the cake as it melts inside my mouth.

Will I share my chocolate cake with him? That's no doubt.
If I can convince him to have one bite he may become hooked
Or maybe he will become just another man in my memory book.

I allowed him to enjoy his strawberry shortcake
While I enjoyed mine.

Hopefully one day we can meet at the same table,
Eat off the same plate
Because we may eventually develop the same taste.

It's truly a blessing to be able to take the covers off of me,
Not being afraid of what you may see, it may or may not
Offend you but it's being free to be me.

So as you read through these pages begin to imagine yourself
Uncovering yourself, allowing you to expose the true essence
Of your beauty
That lies beneath all of the garments.

What's beneath the garments is your skin, beneath your skin
Is the true you that's buried within, so let's begin taking
Off one layer at a time
Undressing the prize.

You can no longer hide.

Under My Safety Tree

As I sat here waiting on you to arrive
Knowing deep inside it can hinder my Prize.
Though I usually play it safe and known for being cautious.
There's a part of me that steps out on the edge
knowing it's a possibility that I can fall!

A kiss is what I fight against
because it can lead me into the bottomless pit.
But when you arrived and began to kiss my lips
rubbing your fingertips across my hips and
caressing my breast.

I thought O What a Mess This Can Be!

But the more you touched me
I became enticed by your Strength,
and the Power of you locking me into position
so out of instincts I gripped my legs around your waist
hoping we can stay in this position forever.
Making love with our clothes on
when we prefer them to be completely off
but realizing.

WE ARE OFF!
Off track.
IF we don't stop now
we should probably fall back!

Reality sets in and we fall asleep.

Wake up
Says our goodbyes and
now we're both feeling empty inside.
But let me Whisper this under my tree
because this space is safe for me.

I know the TRUTH shall MAKE me FREE!

The truth is your erection became a Rejection
because you assumed you caused me to hurt.
But I am not hurt or angered
I lack the touch of a man
That not only my flesh desires but my anointing Requires
the Strength of a Boaz to Protect NOT Reject so I Project that
it's best that I be honest about that night.

That night you do remember?

How have you been I'm not sure but truthfully
do I sound like an angry woman
or could it had been Amazingly Great
to me?

I was Free in the moment but yet
fighting the temptation.

I am Freely Whispering This Under
My Safety Tree...

Overdrawn

I noticed we were out of tissue
Got in my vehicle to go to Dollar General
To pick up four rolls for a dollar
Only to realize I had seventy five cents
Mathematically not adding up to what I needed.

One account was overdrawn by eight dollars
The other overdrawn by eighty cents
No need to panic let's see what's in my savings.
Hurray two dollars and fifty cents!

So I transferred two dollars into my checking account from my savings account,
Only to go into the store for the tissue to cost one dollar and thirty eight cents,
Now I am overdrawn by eighteen cents in my checking account.

Just got through fusing at my son because of his selfishness
Treating me like I'm not worth two cents.

Tears began to moisten my face,
I silently prayed Lord when will I get to a place
That I won't have to taste the bitterness of life?

I mean every spice I have tasted twice.
Even when it's sweet it leaves a bitterness behind
Whatever happened to sugar and spice?
I guess, my spices got twisted.

Mine are more like bitter sweet or
Sour tour for the hour
But the hours last as long as the years
I just cannot seem to stop shedding these tears
I'm overdrawn!

No Stay.
But you do not have on any clothes.

I know, but I am comfortable with them off around you.

Why won't you look at me?
Because you are naked.

O so you're not comfortable with my Nakedness?
Get used to it, I'm no longer hiding!

I said I Do before you asked Will You

I noticed you
Then I looked for you
I soon became distracted by you
I kneeled in prayer to God for you

He revealed things about us
I was impatient
I disregarded what God said to me
By accepting that you had someone else.

Though I moved on
I continued to carry you
Emotionally, Mentally and Spiritually.

I accepted that I was not the one
But one day I was heartbroken and
I dreamed of you
It soothed me and reminded me of what
God told me in regards to us.

You asked me out on a date
God gave me specific instructions to follow
But I disobeyed
Not intentionally
But I was emotionally controlled.

You're one of my first thoughts in the AM,
One of my last thoughts in the PM.

I smile when I think of you
I frown and throw up my hands days thinking of you.
Your Spirit drew me
I dated you way before you asked me out on a date
I held you before you physically wrapped your arms around me.

I kissed you before our truly first kiss
I kissed you Good morning and Good night

I made you soup while you were sick
Yet you never tasted it.

I cooked you breakfast and dinner
I washed your clothes
Though you have not sensed the sweet aroma of the fabric softener
I prayed over you while you were asleep
I held your hand and
I stood by your side.

I encouraged and supported you
I gave you your space when you needed
To be alone
Though you are never alone
Because God and I are
Always with you.

I shared my cares, fears, strengths and weaknesses
I opened the entrance of my heart to you
I submitted and committed myself
To Love you for
Who you are and where you are.

For the record my Love won't ever change
My Love Will Survive Forever
And last a lifetime.

Unconditionally

I was taught unconditional Love by God through two men that never
did much to deserve it
So they say.

They have both questioned "Why does she love me?"

Both not realizing
Love is a choice and
I choose to Love you.

If I can Love you without any reason you can think of
This must be True Love.

I loved things about you,
Then I fell in Love with you
Now I Love you for you.

The question is
Why won't you let me Love you without my Love being questioned by
you?

When I say I Love you I hope my actions are on display
I hope the volume of my actions are to the max
Drowning out my words
I pray that my Love is as soothing
As you soothed me in my dream.

When I say I Love you
It's because I am Love.
You will never find another me
Not a duplicate or a counterfeit.
I Love eternally and externally
My Love extends and expands greatly

I give it in doses
But please whatever you do
Do not overdose!

Here
What?

Put on this.
Why?

Because we are out of bed now.
So.

Well cover up yourself.
We were both naked between the sheets.

Put on your own robe because
I am no longer covering myself up for you.

Married to a Lie

If you think of a lie,
You will tell a lie.

If you will tell a lie,
You will believe a lie.

If you will believe a lie,
You will live a lie.

To divorce is to separate from,
And to be pulled apart
You cannot remarry until
You divorce.

So divorce the lie
To become engage and
Occupy one's self with
The Truth.

I divorced the lies
Became engaged
With the truth and
Now married to He who frees.

It's getting hot in here.
Can I take my shirt off?

Sure.
Thanks.

Now that's more like it.

Relationship Traffic Laws

It is amazing that men are comfortable
Expressing themselves
With a compassionate touch or kiss
And women allows the green light special.

But the moment a woman expresses herself
Outwardly, sharing her inner thoughts and
Her she motions as TD Jakes says it best.

He slams on his emergency brakes
Dropping her off at the nearest stop sign or red light
Saying I've been here before
Same place, different face and
I'm so tired of the chase!

Red means stop.
Green means go.
Yellow means slow.

Let's start obeying relationship traffic laws!

It reminds me of when we walked those school halls
Hearing the teacher saying stop running
Or slow down.

Yes, I am beginning to frown.

Because I ran a few stop signs myself
Sped through the yellow lights
Not paying attention to my speedometer
And took advantage of every green light
Acted as if I was running to catch a flight.
But I realized, the signs are there for many reasons
Though I tried to make you reason with me
Not being patient you see.

I decided to renew my license today

Thank God, I have Blood Insurance
And no tickets to pay.

I was caught by surprise not to have any former DUI's
That's because I know I disobeyed and played
Not by His rules of course.

But today I promise to be cautious, driving for myself
And others.

Men and women are both held accountable
And we will be judged on how we carried His Mantle!

Come have a seat,
Let me help you get comfortable.

Take off your shoes,
Loosen up your tie.

Better yet take it off,
Your shirt too.
While you're at it get naked!

You can no longer mask yourself
Because you are exposed.

Guess what?
I enjoy you better undressed.

De 'sire

I long for my husband
For many reasons
One because it's better to marry
Than to burn.

That is not God's plan
His plan is for he to find she
Not she find he
But he is not ready for me
So what must I do?

I must wait for the date
That is not only in His plan
But in His timing.

Though it's frustrating
Once masturbating and
I know you are relating
To what I am saying.

God honors marriage
I honor God
I wish I can find
The answer on his IPod.

But though it tarry
I will wait
I won't break
Fall or bend.

Because what was the Purpose of being celibate?
Overall to be free of sin.

I discovered your uniqueness.
You have a dimple on your left cheek.

I know, please do not tell anyone.
I hate it!

Why?
Because.

Well, I find it to be tasteful.

Now I cannot pay him to put his clothes on when he is around me.

<u>Deja' Vu</u>

I want you, but you don't want me.
He wants me, but I don't want him.
She wants him, but he does not want her.
You want her, but she does not want you.
Could this be Deja' Vu?

You want her but she wants him.
He wants her but she wants he.
She wants him but he wants she.
He wants me but I want you.
Could this be Deja' Vu?

The she is not me.
The he is not you.
Could this be Deja' Vu?

You chase her.
She chases him.
He chases me.
I chase you.
Could this be Deja' Vu?

Never seeming to love the one who loves you
This happens to be real life shared between two.

Men want to be able to get naked and honest too.
Stop making him cover up his hurt and fears
As his dad did.

Or being a duplicate of what his father was
Make him as comfortable as you can when he is in your presence
That's truly what makes you different.

Listen Up

I heard you but I did not listen
Yes, I know there's a difference.

But after I replayed everything you said
I began to understand what I missed.

I missed the fact that you said,
"It won't change our status."
And you are not ready for a relationship,
With me of course.

Not to mention the lie you were out of town
Only for me to drive by your house
To realize you wasn't.

But I am not mad at you
I'm just listening and paying close attention
So I do not continue to ignore
The words that are flowing out of your mouth.

Though your actions for months now
Says something totally different
I guess, that's why I was confused.

But I am here to share the news
You have my undivided attention because
Now I am finally listening.

Before exposing yourself to someone else,
Expose yourself to yourself.

Are you attracted to yourself?
Now that's what matters.

Dos and Don'ts

I don't need you to say you admire me
I tell myself that daily.

I don't need you to say you adore me
Instead show me

I don't want you to lie to me or even lie for me
Because I live by the Truth.

I do need your respect, protection and support.

Value me and my opinions
You can do as I say and/or as I do.

Because they both will always
Be the right guidance for you.

I am always striving to do the right thing.

Skin test
Are you comfortable in it?

Special Delivery

I was surprised to receive a message in my in-box,
Eagerly to read
Yes, indeed.

O how nice!
What did I do to deserve this?
Being the woman I am, I guess.

Could this be a test?
I must thank him in my own way
He left his number perhaps I will call him someday.

Why put it off until tomorrow?
A day that's not promised.
What the heck I will send mine too.
What's the harm in it?

He called.
We laughed.
Eventually time passed.

It's was late,
Time to close
He said good night but was wondering what the future holds.

A reason, season or lifetime no one knows?
The present is for sure
It's an open door

Yes, friendship guaranteed
Rest my friend you're in safe hands with me.

I dare you!
To become bare.

Keeping His Day Holy

Hey can we do it?
Do what?
Do it.
Sure.

What time should I expect you?
After Bible Study.
No, that won't be good!
Why not?
Because Bishop Bronner is preaching on TEMPTATION!

O it's okay to sin Monday through Wednesday
But skip Thursday due to Bible Study.
Pick back up Friday and Saturday
But No sex on Sunday.

I mean, excuse me for sharing my viewpoint of this
But God hates sin!
He can careless the day the sin is committed on but
He hates the sin!

Imagine an alcoholic saying, I will get drunk but never on Sunday.
A drug addict saying, I get high but I reverence the Lord's Day.

Are you serious?
The last I checked,
Every day belongs to the Lord.

This is the day that the Lord has made;
We shall rejoice and be glad in it.

Well, after hearing the word on temptation, I called him up
Can I speak with you?
Yes, of course.
I am on my way.
Okay.

I'm trying to draw the line in the sand with this man
Because he has no intentions on making this an "Us"
I explained my pain,
Which gave me chills.

Constantly reminded myself these were the cards I dealt.

He respectfully said, "Okay
You will be missed."

Reverencing the Lord's Day by hitting the highway
It's time to Honor every day He has made!

Men make her just as comfortable without it.
Make- up is to enhance her.
Not make her!

Why Did You Wake Her?

She was asleep for seven years and six months
Bothering no one
But you came along trying to wake her
She had been in a coma state for years
I kept telling you let her rest
But you insisted on ignoring me.

Shhhh she's sleeping.

IF you wake her
Well, let me warn you
She will need a lot of attention
The attention she requires
Well, you might want to just let her be because
I am not sure you are able to tend to me.

I was able to see about myself for many years
But that no longer works for me so
Please do us both a favor and let me be.

Yes, I am repeating myself
Please stop touching her!
She won't know how to act.

O it feels so good please, stop please
He is kissing her
O no he is waking her
Now she's awake and wants to play!

But he says
Game over!

She's dripping wet in tears and he leaves her there
High and dry
Saying goodbye.

She's now wide awake

Wanting to play.

Many are around and don't mind showing her attention
But she likes the games he played with her
Why did he wake her in the first place?
Now she has to break down and masturbate.

To kill the craving
Of him laying inside her for just that one time
Stroking her from behind
That's all she seems to remember of the past.

She keeps reminiscing on how long and strong he was
So stimulating that it caused her twin towers to stand at attention!
But now he gives her no attention at all.

He said, "I'm done. I suggest you go back to sleep!"

Believing has kept me Breathing

I believe I am a compassionate person.
I believe I have a huge heart.
I believe I am an obedient child.
I believe I am a wise parent.
I believe I am a loving grandparent.

I believe I am success.
I believe I am rich.
I believe I am a testimony.
I believe I serve an Awesome God.
I believe I am an overcomer.

I believe I will speak to the nation.
I believe I am a wife.
I believe I am a poet.
I believe I am a life coach.
I believe I am a prophet.

I believe, yes I do believe!

I believe I am a dreamer.
I believe dreams are possible
To him who believes.

I believe I am who I say I am.
So as a man think so is he.
I believe my words are powerful.
I believe I speak to my future.
I believe it does what I say.

I believe I am a business owner.
I believe I am trained to manage.
I believe I am skilled to supervise.
I believe I am a leader,
Who leads many to Christ.

In believing,

If nothing come to pass
Knowing God can
Is what I need to in order to
Breathe again!

It's my right to Believe.

I apologize.
For?

I saw you naked.
You did?

What did you see?
Your beauty was shared with me.

How did you feel?
I did not want to shut my eyes.

Why did you?
I did not want to be caught by you.

Why not?
Because I thought I invaded your privacy.

Actually, I knew you were there all along.

Silent Goodbyes

It was just yesterday
When you asked me to come over and play
The other night when we had
A small cat fight.

The apologies were sent through texts

But I did not get the telegram
That you wanted your space
Maybe it's you wanting me replaced
Though I know we are both in different places
I hate rejection of any case.

I went on a fast seeking God in this
I promised, I won't continue on this way
Any longer.

I could have called and shared the news
But instead I waited for you to
I realized that day will never come
So I silently sent my voice that you hear
In the late night hour
Right after your shower.

While you're lying alone
Not conversing on the phone
Yes, without any distractions.

You have a thought
About the time we've shared
Probably around the same time
I'm starring at the walls
I picked up my phone
You picked up yours.

Then we both silently say no more
And send our silent Goodbyes

Goodbye my love; Goodbye…

Being uncovered
Makes one feel unprotected.

But the true protection is being uncovered.

I'm nearly naked now,
I do not care who sees me.

I'm sure if I walk outdoors
The neighbors will call the police.

And I will only get a ticket.
To be honest, this ticket will be
Worth paying for.

Turning Back the Hands of Time

I had a head on collision with my past today
It showed me what my present could have been
Though I cannot change my past
If that was at all possible
Having to go through all the hell I went through
I would have chosen to endured it with you

All I can say is where were you all of those days?

I was not the only one who remembered you
When seeing your face after you shouted out my name
My heart skipped a beat and screamed
"I remember him!"

I know there's no way we can recapture those years
But you gave me hope for my future
Seeing you made me believe
That I will soon find love again or
It will soon find me.

This is not a strip tease
As you can see.
Are you afraid to join me?

My Good Mornings have Meaning

When I say Good morning
I'm saying, thank you God for waking him.

When I say Good afternoon
I'm saying, thank you God for keeping him throughout the day.

When I say Good night
I'm saying, Lord Please Protect him during the night
So I can say Good morning once again.

Good morning my love, my prayers have been answered.

Your friend.

Take it off.

Blinded By Your Own View

You do not love me the way that I love you
You do not perceive me the way that I perceive you
Stand over here and hopefully
You can see more clearly.

After changing positions with you I noticed
Every time I detect a light from afar
Someone comes along and blindfold me
Blocking the view of you and me.

Sorry but I cannot perceive you differently
My love cannot be compared to yours either
But though we have different views
I do love you.

I must admit after I stepped into your shadow
The shade began to fade
And the light began to shine
Though it's still hard for us to intertwine
I realized that maybe it's time for me to take off the blindfold.

Take it all off!

Your First Born

Every man deserves a son
If not two just one.

I pictured your first born,
I remembered you expressing your heart was once torn.

But I promise
The blood that flows through his veins
Are yours,

When you witness his first kick
And hold him for the first time
I pray this will be a reminder of
God's Mercy, Grace, Healing and Favor.

In replace of the sorrows and the hurt
Not to mention the shame.
He will carry your entire name
Because he is a reflection of your love
Not your pain!

Your Son, Your Name, Your Gift, Your Gain

Yours truly.

Uncovering what once had me buried.

Make Love to Me

When I say make love to me
I'm saying, you're pregnant with a vision.

When I say make love to me
I'm saying, I'm open to receive you.

When I say make love to me
I'm saying, I'm ready to nurture what's in you.

When I say make love to me
I'm saying
Pour out of you
By releasing into me
Because I am wide open to receive
What is inside of you.

I promise to conceive and carry the vision
That was birthed in you full term
So it can be a healthy delivery through me.

Son of God, Man of God and King
Make love to me!

Now, I can see you
From all angles.

Why?

Now I lay my body to sleep,
I pray the Lord my soul to keep.

If I should die before I awake
Go by his house and complete a heart surgery.

Taking my heart and replacing his with mine,
While you're at it exchange our minds.

So he will contemplate on every one
Of my thoughts of him
And finally relate with my feelings for him.

Then he won't be left wondering
Why did she love me the way she did?

He will know
Why I loved him?
And how much
He was loved.

I am finally free to expose
The real me.

Shakisha Uncovered

I do not have a degree nor do I have a PhD
Not even a diploma for that matter
More like a G.E.D.

But is that what truly defines me?
Am I defined by the material things of the world?
Am I truly a material girl?

No not at all!
The world does not define who I am.

Seriously at one point I've tried to keep up with their trends
But the more I bend
The more I lose
Loss my virginity way too soon.

Thirteen is when I made that choice
No force used by this dude

The force of trying to fit in
Feeling left out I began to pout
Fell into a trap and can't bounce back.

So the enemy thought!

He set his trap but God had a plan
A plan for my life; whole time I was in His hand.
He said, "The Good and the bad works together for
The good of those who love Him and to whom which
Are called according to His purpose."

O my bad for quoting scriptures
My Good for being raised in the hood
You see how twisted the people in this world are!

Gave birth to my first born at fifteen
A child raising a baby; yea that was me

She weighed seven pounds and fourteen ounces
As beautiful as she can be
But what can I offer her?
Thinking all she needed was me.

The first time her dad met her was through a portrait
Can you picture that?
Half of her life cursed by me and abandoned by him
But we want her to become our gem.

Gemstone is what I am referring to
A gem is a precious stone
Anything prized for its value.

At sixteen the abortion table was calling me
How sick can this be?
So sick my mother will chance us being homeless
Before she'll risk me raising a nursery.

Those were her words towards me that made me hate her for years
But I never understood her tears
Unaware of her true fears of me repeating
This vicious cycle!

She wanted the best for me
I chose more babies!
Searching for love they say
Really!

No, more like living out the legacy that was before me
Before meaning in front of me
What did I see?

My step dad beat me
No not me, she
Who is she?
My mommy!

I saw her black eyes and busted lips,

I heard her pleading for her life,
I witnessed her grabbing knives to defend herself
He chased us out the room with a belt
Who really needs a beaten here?

Daddy why do you beat mommy?
Because I love her he replies.
Mommy why do you stay with daddy?
For my children; that's why.
But baby girl never be with a man who beats you!

This is what I call the Belt of Truth!

I witnessed the first crack pipe to my father's lips,
The first fist was his into my mother's lips.
O not to mention the first moan and groan.

What's that?
The sound of sex coming from the other side of my mother's closed
bedroom door

Don't get it twisted she was no man's whore!
But at this time no man's wife either.

She cooked and cleaned
He paid all of the bills
From the outside looking in you would think we lived in Beverly Hills
But I plead to differ more like Living in Color
The black and the grays described my days.

Anyone hungry yet?

Woke up at 3am in the morning,
Nothing to eat and
Parents were extremely geek!

I began to cry,
Daddy noticed my tears,
He neglected the drugs to care for me.

He took me to seven eleven,
To get me a cold turkey sandwich but
I complained not because I was hungry.

Hungry for what?
Hungry for change!

Having my third child but second born
At seventeen my life was torn
Torn apart; torn to pieces
But you knew he were no good!

He blacked my eyes, busted my lips, spit in my face
Perhaps you should just take that trip
Trip to where?
What place?

O No! This was not her fault.
I did this to myself
So I owe her a chance.
A chance at what?

Not sure.
But I would rather take a risk on raising that nursery, than to go back
into surgery
Causing death upon my unborn
Maybe just maybe she'll have a better chance who knows?

A better chance at life.
Really?

What will she do differently?

I don't know but I have faith
That I will soon rise up from this place
Seeing my children make better decisions
So they won't have to suffer the same consequences
Or continue to repeat the vicious cycle.

Because life is not always as enjoyable as it was
When I was riding my bicycle
Yes, having no worries at all.
But every now and again you will have a fall

You will get back up again and start over
That's exactly what I've been doing
Now I have closure because
God defines the true beauty of me from within!
Shakisha gives thanks to God for ending the wick-Edness

As she now embraces her Gift-Edness!

I hope you like
What you see
Because this is truly
The Naked side of me!

About the Author

SHAKISHA SHAMAIN EDNESS, a writer, mentor, motivational speaker and evangelist for Christ. Speaking Truth, Changing Perception, and Gaining Lives to Christ by sharing her testimonies and word of God. She is from Newark, New Jersey and partially raised in Atlanta, Georgia. She found her passion through her pain, and then her pain directed her to her God's given purpose. She is truly an inspiration to others and she gives all the recognitions to Jesus!

Author Contact Information

To purchase books, for more information, or to schedule Shakisha
Edness to speak, please contact:

Shakisha Edness

www.shakishaedness.com

www.ingramcontent.com/pod-product-compliance
Lightning Source LLC
LaVergne TN
LVHW051815080426
835513LV00017B/1973